MILITARY DOGS
ON THE JOB

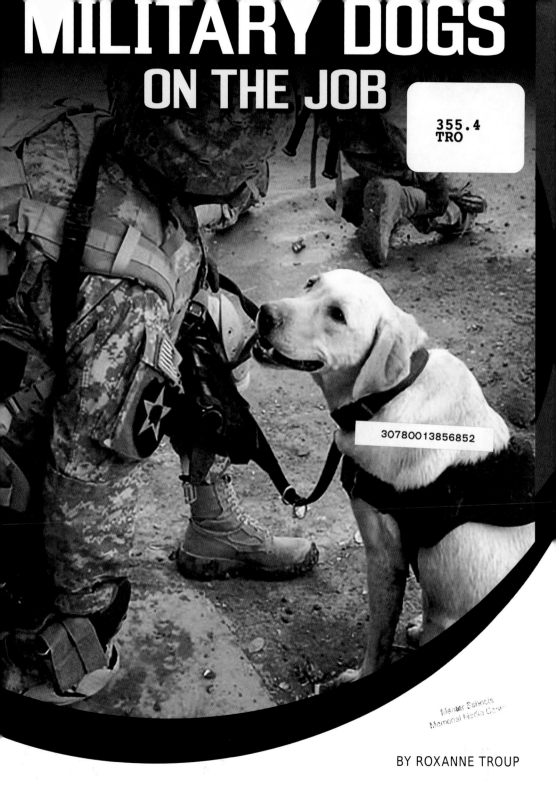

BY ROXANNE TROUP

Published by The Child's World®
1980 Lookout Drive • Mankato, MN 56003-1705
800-599-READ • www.childsworld.com

Photographs ©: Staff Sgt. Stacy L. Pearsall/U.S. Air Force, cover, 1; Sgt. Bobby J. Yarbrough/DVIDS, 5; Senior Airman Eric Harris/DVIDS, 6; Cpl. Alejandro Pena/U.S. Marine Corps, 8; U.S. Army, 9; Spc. Jennifer Grier/ DVIDS, 10; Cpl. Alejandro Pena/U.S. Air Force, 12; Senior Airman Meagan Schutter/U.S. Air Force, 13; Staff Sgt. Taresha Hill/DVIDS, 14; Lance Cpl. Zachery B. Martin/U.S. Marine Corps, 17; Kurt Gibbons III/UPI Photo/ Newscom, 18; Cpl. Jennifer Pirante/DVIDS, 20

ISBN 9781503816138

LCCN 2016945860

Printed in the United States of America
PA02318

TABLE OF
CONTENTS

FAST FACTS

The Job

- Military Working Dogs (MWDs) patrol military bases. The dogs protect their **handlers**.
- Military dogs are used to find hidden bombs, drugs, and weapons.
- The dogs are also used to find and track people.

Training Time

- MWDs are **fostered** until they are seven months old. Fostering helps dogs feel comfortable in different places.
- Dogs start their training by learning **obedience**. It takes seven to 11 weeks to teach dogs to listen to and obey their handlers.
- After learning to obey, dogs start working on special skills. Special training lasts four to six weeks.

Common Breeds

- Belgian Malinois
- German and Dutch shepherds
- Labrador and golden retrievers

Famous Dogs

- Stubby served in World War I (1914–1918) as a guard dog. He was the first dog to be given a rank in the U.S. military.

- Chips served during World War II (1939–1945). He carried equipment through dangerous areas and helped soldiers capture enemy fighters.

- Cairo was a member of the Navy SEALs. In 2011, he helped find the terrorist Osama bin Laden.

Chapter 1

LEADING THE WAY

Training was over. It was time for Lucca to go to work. Her first mission was to search for homemade bombs called IEDs. During the Afghanistan War (2001–2014), these bombs were buried by roads and in fields. The bombs often **detonated** without warning and hurt people. But Lucca could smell them. The soldiers with Lucca relied on her to keep them safe.

On command, Lucca began searching. With her nose to the ground, she zigzagged up the road in front of the soldiers. The soldiers were nearing a town. Lucca sped up. She could smell something ahead.

Back and forth Lucca went, looking for where the scent was strongest. Lucca walked toward a **compound**.

◀ **Lucca worked on more than 400 missions in the Middle East.**

▲ **A military dog searches near a road. Dogs can help make sure roads are safe for vehicles to drive on.**

Lucca seemed to think something was hidden there. Lucca's handler kept a close eye on Lucca. He was looking for her to signal that she had found something.

Lucca came close to the compound walls. Her zigzagging slowed. Each time she turned, she took fewer steps. Her tail twitched. Lucca's handler knew Lucca could smell something. Suddenly Lucca stopped. She started to sit. It was the sign the soldier had been waiting for.

▲ IEDs are often buried under debris, making them difficult for people to identify.

Chapter 2

BEFORE THE MISSION

The military uses many dogs like Lucca. These dogs are not soldier's pets. They are Military Working Dogs (MWDs). Training starts early for these special dogs.

A MWD puppy gets lots of attention. Trainers tickle and hold him. They give him toys to chew on and chase. The trainers encourage the puppy to use his **instincts**. Soon the puppy goes to live with a foster family. This is to help him get used to being around different people.

The foster family takes care of the puppy. They bring him to the grocery store and to soccer games. The family lets the puppy ride in the car. The puppy experiences many different places, smells, and sounds. At seven months, the puppy starts obedience training.

◄ **Military puppies are exposed to many new people. This helps them get used to new situations.**

▲ Trainers use toys to make training fun for dogs.

During obedience training, the dog learns to stay on task. He learns to listen to his handler's commands. Dogs and handlers train together for 16 weeks to become a team.

On the first day of training, the dog gets a hollow ball to chew on and carry around. Handlers use the rubber balls to teach their dogs how to search. Later the toy will be the puppy's reward for finding hidden objects.

A handler hides a young German shepherd's ball in another room. The dog sniffs around, slowly moving toward the room. Soon the dog finds the ball and brings it back to his handler. The handler hides it again, this time in a cabinet. The dog cannot see his ball, but he can smell it. He starts searching with his nose in the air. He does not stop until he finds his favorite toy.

▲ **Military dogs quickly learn to find their toys even when the toys are out of sight.**

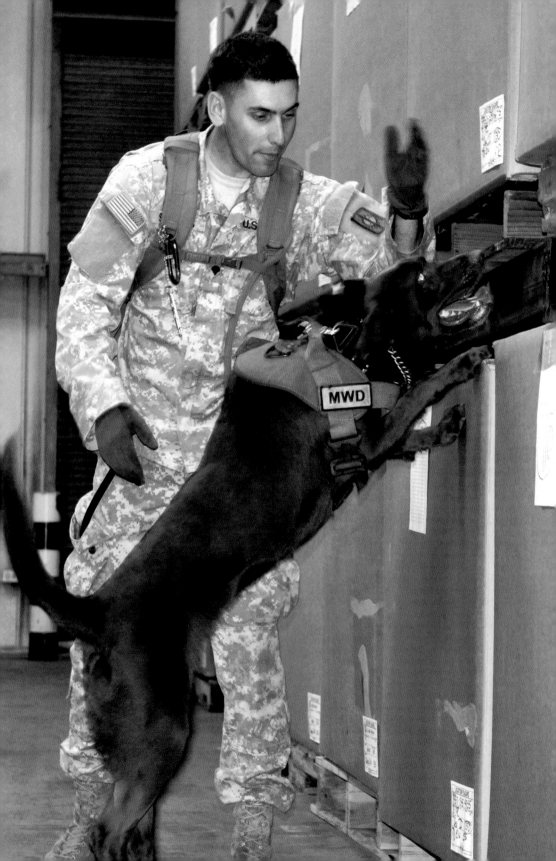

After the German shepherd is trained with a ball, his handler brings him outside. The handler puts a smelly rag under the dog's nose. The dog has never smelled the odor before. The handler takes away the rag and tells the dog to search. The German shepherd sniffs the air. He turns in the direction of the new smell. He sniffs again, this time on the ground. He moves closer to the smell. The dog keeps sniffing. If he finds the smell again, he can play with his ball. It takes a few tries, but soon the dog finds the smell under a rock. After nine weeks, he can find nine different odors.

In order to complete special training, MWD teams have to take a test. During testing, the dog and its handler look for nine different odors. They look in buildings and cars. They look in fields. They even look in theaters full of people. The dog can make only one mistake if it is going to pass the test.

◀ **Handlers and dogs take tests together before they become official teams.**

After testing, teams travel to Arizona for their last simulation. Since many MWDs are **deployed** to the Middle East, they need to practice somewhere hot. The deserts of Arizona are very hot. For two weeks, teams practice in their new location. They work on a skill called birding.

Birding lets dogs work faster. During birding, handlers look for places bombs could be hidden. They unleash their dogs and direct them with voice commands. Without their leashes, dogs can search for the familiar smells of bombs without waiting for their handlers to catch up.

A Labrador retriever is birding. Her handler unclips her leash. The handler calls out, "Seek." The Labrador begins sniffing the air for one of the odors she has learned to recognize. The handler calls out again, "Left!" The Lab turns left and keeps sniffing. "Right," the handler yells. The dog turns right. She walks a little farther and stops. She sniffs the ground and sits down.

▲ Dogs must listen closely to their handler's commands when off their leashes.

"Come," her handler calls, and the dog returns. The handler praises the Lab. She found what they were looking for.

After training, MWD teams are assigned to local military bases or deployed overseas. Wherever they go, the dog and handler practice their skills every day.

Chapter 3

AFTER THE MISSION

Lucca's ears perked up. "Come, Lucca!" her handler called. Lucca ran back to her handler with her tail wagging. Her handler rubbed Lucca's face and patted her back. But he could not give her a toy. It was still too dangerous. Instead Lucca's handler showed their **platoon** leader what she had found. It looked like a pile of trash with rocks and weeds mixed in.

The platoon leader moved everyone back. He called in bomb experts, just in case Lucca had found an IED. From a safe distance, the experts shot water at the pile. They wanted to push the trash aside and see what was underneath.

◀ Bomb experts can use robots and other methods to examine potential explosive devices from far away.

▲ Lucca lost one of her front legs from an injury in 2012, but she continued to help soldiers away from the battlefield.

Suddenly a huge blast shook the ground where the platoon stood. The trash was gone. In its place was a crater big enough to hide a small car! None of the soldiers were hurt. Lucca had saved an entire platoon!

Lucca and other military dogs help make soldiers' jobs easier. They can also help soldiers who have been to war settle back into normal life.

When Lucca **retired** from the military, her handler adopted her. She lived with his family as their pet. She also helped other soldiers. Her handler took Lucca to visit soldiers who were hurt during war. Lucca was also hurt in the line of duty. Lucca helped cheer up soldiers. She was an **inspiration** both on the front lines and back home.

THINK ABOUT IT

- What things can dogs do that make them great soldiers?
- Most soldiers start training after the age of 18. Why do military working dogs have to start training as puppies?
- To MWDs, their job is a game. How do handlers reward their dogs for a job well done?
- Handlers spend a lot of time training their dogs. What special things would you like to train a dog to do?

GLOSSARY

compound (KAHM-pownd): A compound is an area of land that is fenced in and contains one or more buildings. Lucca searched around a compound for hidden bombs.

deployed (di-PLOYD): To be deployed means to be sent into battle. Many soldiers were deployed in the early 2000s.

detonated (DET-uh-nate-ed): To be detonated means to be exploded. The bomb experts detonated the bomb.

fostered (FAWS-turd): To be fostered is to be raised by temporary owners. Military dogs are fostered by families.

handlers (HAND-lurs): Handlers are people who train animals. The handlers taught the puppies to sit.

inspiration (in-spuh-RAY-shuhn): An inspiration is a person or thing that inspires or encourages someone else. Lucca was an inspiration to the soldiers who had lost their legs.

instincts (IN-stingkts): Instincts are natural animal behaviors. When threatened, a dog's instincts tell it to fight.

obedience (oh-BEE-dee-ens): Obedience is the act of following directions. Puppies first learn obedience.

platoon (pluh-TOON): A platoon is a large group of soldiers. A platoon of 30 soldiers marched down the road.

retired (ri-TIRED): To be retired is to have stopped working. Lucca retired after she got hurt.

TO LEARN MORE

Books

Furstinger, Nancy. *Paws of Courage*. Washington, DC: National Geographic, 2016.

Goldish, Meish. *War Dogs*. New York: Bearport, 2012.

Patent, Dorothy Hinshaw. *Dogs on Duty*. New York: Walker, 2012.

Web Sites

Visit our Web site for links about military dogs: childsworld.com/links

Note to Parents, Teachers, and Librarians: We routinely verify our Web links to make sure they are safe and active sites. So encourage your readers to check them out!

SELECTED BIBLIOGRAPHY

Frankel, Rebecca. *War Dogs*. New York: Palgrave Macmillan, 2014. Print.

Goodavage, Maria. *Top Dog*. New York: Dutton, 2014. Print.

McClellan, Max. "Sniffing for Bombs: Meet America's Most Elite Dogs." *60 Minutes*. CBS Interactive, 22 Apr. 2013. Web. 5 Jul. 2016.

Ritland, Mike. *Navy SEAL Dogs*. New York: St. Martin's, 2013. Print.

INDEX

ABOUT THE AUTHOR

With a background in elementary education, Roxanne Troup writes engaging nonfiction for children of all ages. Her work has appeared in a variety of magazines, including *Boys Quest* and *Christian Home and School*. She and her husband live in Colorado Springs, Colorado, with their three children.